'60s

FLASHBACK

Music Collectibles from the Age of Change

'60s FLASHBACK

Music Collectibles from the Age of Change

Greg Paul

Library of
Applied Design

AN IMPRINT OF

PBC INTERNATIONAL, INC.

Distributor to the book trade in the United States and Canada
Rizzoli International Publications Inc.
300 Park Avenue South
New York, NY 10010

Distributor to the art trade in the United States and Canada
PBC International, Inc.
One School Street
Glen Cove, NY 11542

Distributor throughout the rest of the world
Hearst Books International
1350 Avenue of the Americas
New York, NY 10019

Library of Congress Cataloging–in–Publication Data

'60s Flashback : music collectibles from the age of change / by Greg Paul.
      p.   cm.
   Includes index.
   ISBN 0–86636–279–7
   1. Popular music—1961–1970—Pictorial works. 2. Graphic arts.
3. Popular music—1961–1970—Collectibles.   I. Title
ML3470.P38 1995   94–35574
781.64—dc20   CIP
                           MN

CAVEAT– Information in this text is believed accurate, and will pose no problem for the student or casual reader. However, the author was often constrained by information contained in signed release forms, information that could have been in error or not included at all. Any misinformation (or lack of information) is the result of failure in these attestations. The author has done whatever is possible to insure accuracy.

Color separation by Fine Arts Repro House Co., Ltd., H.K.
Printing and binding by Toppan Printing Co., H.K.

Design: Garrett Schuh

10 9 8 7 6 5 4 3 2 1

Printed in Hong Kong

Table of Contents

FOREWORD

Peter Noone

Peter Noone is the legendary lead
vocalist of Herman's Hermits and is
host of VH-1's "My Generation."
He tours the world in concert, and
continues to grow with a busy stage,
screen and television career.

What a fabulous surprise I had when I first looked through this collection and found it was a pictorial voyage through "My Generation."

You didn't have to have been around in the 60s to know or be excited by this work because, amazingly, it's still around, and for some strange reason, it's just as exciting to look at today as it was thirty years ago.

I was never much into nostalgia, but this collection made me nostalgic for the Fab Four, Cream, Zeppelin, Zappa, Hendrix, and more. Several of my friends have previewed this collection and not one has been able to flip through without stopping, pointing and saying "I remember that!" There's a memory in every piece.

If you were there, you too will remember this incredible time with every page you turn. And if you weren't, you now have a chance to experience this era—to put pictures with music and finally look at what you may have until now only heard.

What a splendid time we all had...I sound like my dad!

INTRODUCTION

Greg Paul

Conventional wisdom divides '60s pop music history into two rather arbitrary and lopsided segments: pre-Beatles schlock, and post-Beatles "rock." It is a simple, if obvious, organizing principle, but one that is useful for only the most superficial of musical discussions. To categorize the pre-Beatles '60s as a vast wasteland of pre-fab teen idols and payola-addled deejays is a short-sighted oversimplification.

While early '60s rock 'n' roll fans were disheartened at finding Elvis in the Army, Chuck Berry in jail, Alan Freed in the unemployment line, and Buddy Holly in his grave, there were numerous signs of renewal and continued vitality on the jazz and rhythm and blues charts. Seminal artists like James Brown, Ray Charles, Sam Cooke, Etta James, Muddy Waters and Jackie Wilson were doing some of their best work at the dawn of the decade.

It was in 1960 that Berry Gordy launched the soon-to-be-legendary Motown label, joining a growing list of daring independents including Atlantic, King, Chess, Vee-Jay, Duke, Imperial and Blue Note. In the period between 1960 and the 1964 British invasion, Bob Dylan, Phil Spector, Brian Wilson, Smokey Robinson, Aretha Franklin, Otis Redding and Stevie Wonder all began recording careers destined to reach deep into the post-Beatles '60s.

If the phenomenal artistic and commercial success of the Beatles and Rolling Stones was not a turning point, it certainly provides a convenient milepost marking that brief season when the "passing fad" known as rock 'n' roll suddenly galvanized an entire generation, tangled itself inextricably with that generation's fashions, politics, hopes and dreams—in fact, becoming an indelible part of their very identity—to emerge as the self-conscious art form known as "rock."

For our survey of '60s pop music memorabilia, we have employed the arbitrary cut-off dates of January 1959 through December 1970. A year was added at the front end in order to bring in a little more of the late '50s flavor that was so prevalent in the early '60s, and because things do not change overnight. By extending the deadline through 1970 we are able to encompass such important decade-enders as the release of the Woodstock movie and LP, the Kent State shootings, the Beatles breakup, and the deaths of Jimi Hendrix and Janis Joplin.

The pop artifacts presented here are not the rare and expensive one-of-a-kind mementos often sold at auction or displayed at the Hard Rock Cafes. Do not look here for John Lennon's glasses or Robert Plant's pink Cadillac. Our featured collectibles were all mass-produced, and excepting the guitars, are quite affordable, even today.

Throughout the '60s printing presses churned out album jackets, record sleeves and labels, concert tickets, posters, buttons and handbills by the millions. Because so much of the memorabilia featured here was produced on the printing press, this book is a de facto document of '60s graphic design and packaging as it relates to popular music.

In 1960, graphic design was a small and somewhat elitist offshoot of a craft commonly known as commercial art. Corporate annual reports, museums, galleries, modern jazz and serious music got the graphic design treatment, leaving the packaging and advertising of everything else (including rock 'n' roll) to the naive and unpretentious, but often crass devices of the commercial artist. As the decade progressed graphic design grew in importance and influence, egged on by a younger, more visually aware generation that had been weaned on television and Technicolor movies, and had developed an appetite for daring and sophisticated graphics. By 1970 the print-shop-trained commercial artist, so dominant early in the decade, was being phased out, a victim of the trend toward the more-studied visual style of the college educated graphic designers.

Coming into the '60s, classical, jazz and to a lesser degree folk music, had already achieved the status of serious art, and this attitude was reflected in the reverent graphics used for their packaging and promotion. Rock 'n' roll, rhythm and blues, country western, and novelty tunes, however, were another matter; considered lowbrow product, they were cheaply packaged for consumption by the unwashed masses. But by

mid-decade change was in the wind. Critics and scholars suddenly began waxing poetic about pop music and pop culture in general. Even serious music maven Leonard Bernstein confessed to millions in his TV audience that he was a fan of the Beach Boys. Rock 'n' roll was now legitimate art, and hence-forth would require the attentions of the burgeoning graphic design community for its packaging and marketing.

So it was that pop music and graphic design evolved simultaneously. Evidence of their parallel development can be found in the increased use of producer and designer credits. Both are absent from most album jackets circa 1960 but by 1970 their inclusion had become standard practice.

In these pages we are able to witness pop music's journey from the naive to the self-conscious, and its eventual splintering into myriad subsets (garage rock, bubblegum, folk rock, heavy metal, etc.) aided and abetted by that curious blend of hype and artistry known as modern graphic design.

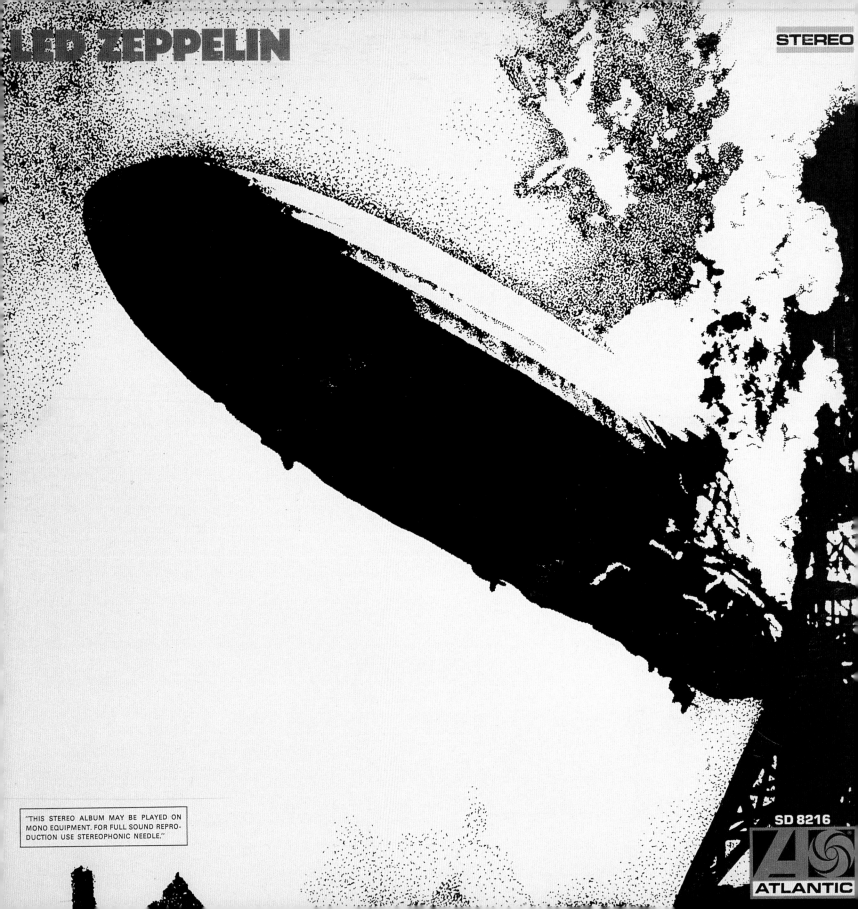

Overview

We begin with a showcase of quintessential '60s images. Many of these items were ubiquitous throughout the decade, some attaining the status of icons. It is a testament to the power of our deeply ingrained disposable culture that so many could become rare and collectible today.

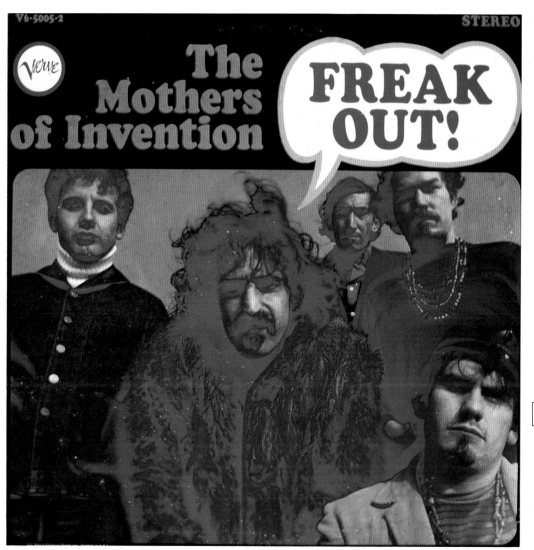

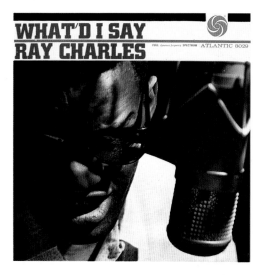

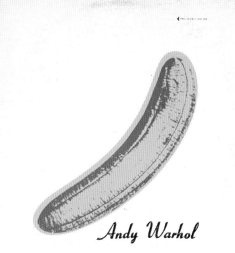

One of the premier '60s guitars, this 1959 Gibson Les Paul was reissued in 1982 at the special request of Leo's Guitar Shop in Oakland, California.

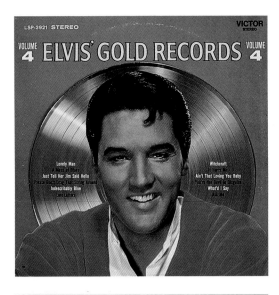

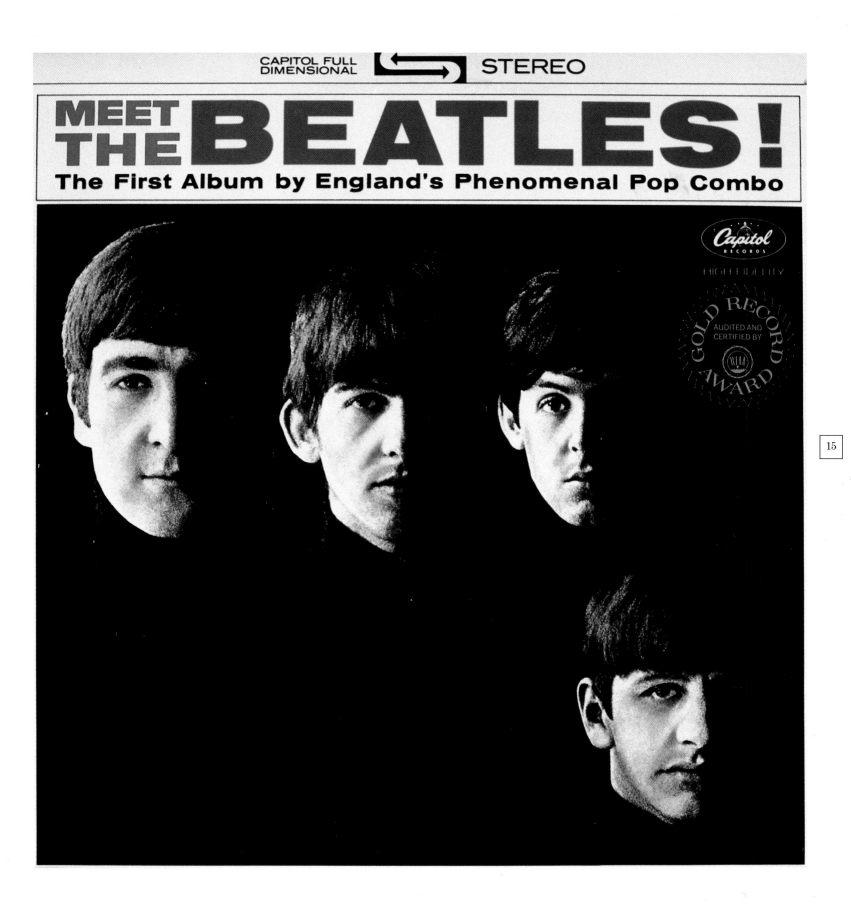

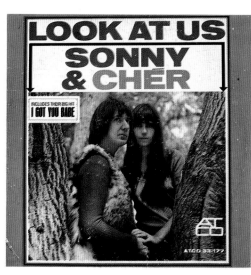

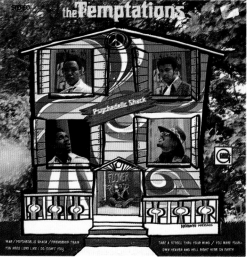

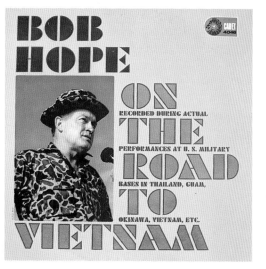

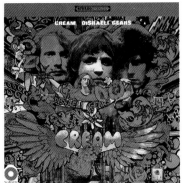

It's hard to imagine rock 'n' roll without the Fender Stratocaster. This is the axe most favored by '60s guitar legends Eric Clapton and Jimi Hendrix. The model shown hails from 1958 and sports a blonde custom color and maple neck.

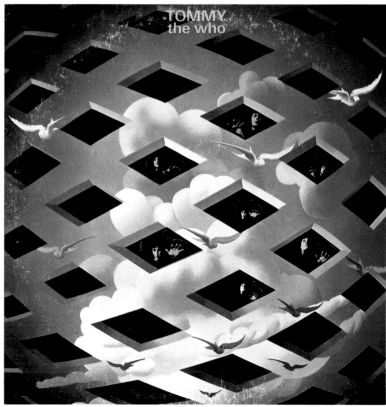

21

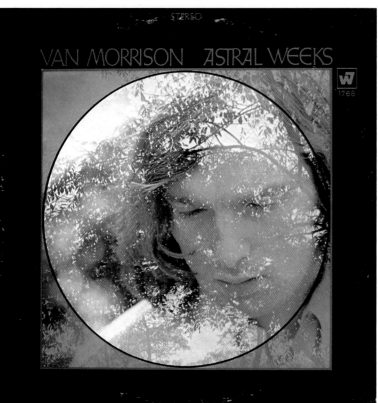

Fender's electric Jazz Bass revolutionized rock 'n' roll. Bass players readily traded the natural woody tone of the acoustic bass viol for the added decibels of the bass guitar. Depicted is a rare 1962 model in Olympic white custom color.

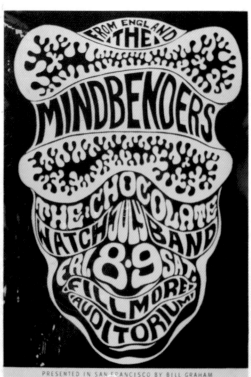

The Rickenbacker
12 string electric
(model shown is a
1967 360/12OS
autographed by
Roger McGuinn)
provided the
patented jangly
guitar sound of
the Byrds and
Beatles.

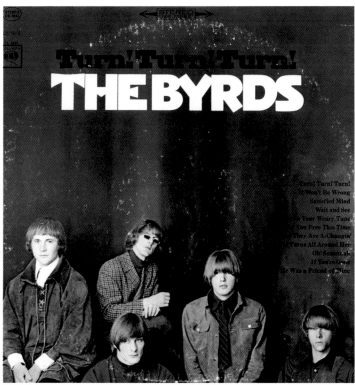

DIPLOMAT STEREO —FM 100

THE TWIST

THE TWIST

THE TWIST

TWISTIN' • DOIN' THE TWIST • STAND AROUND, MOVE AROUND • GOIN' STEADY • COME TWIST WITH ME •

SPEARMINT TWIST • NEW YORK CITY TWIST • CANDYBAR • I REALLY LOVE THE TWIST • TWISTIN' OUT OF SPACE

Land of a Thousand Dances

The Twist was quite simply the biggest dance craze ever. While Chubby Checker and Joey Dee became household names, everybody from Ray Charles to Lester Lanin put out Twist records. Instantly, the race was on to foster the next great dance craze. Even jazz artists like Ray Bryant and Ernie Freeman got in on the act. The Boogaloo, Hully Gully, Watusi, Locomotion and countless others came and went, none ever replicating the Twist's unprecedented popularity.

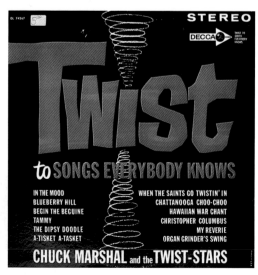

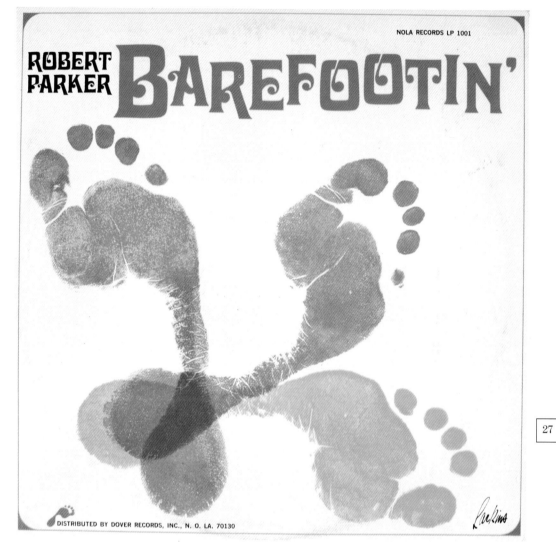

RCA
CAS-2304

CAMDEN
STEREO

ELVIS SINGS FLAMING STAR

Wonderful World
Night Life
All I Needed Was the Rain
Too Much Monkey Business
Yellow Rose of Texas
The Eyes of Texas
She's a Machine
Do the Vega
Tiger Man

Teen Idols

At the dawn of the '60s the entertainment industry continued its desperate search for the next Elvis, still not hip to the fact that real stars are born, not made.

A few talented holdovers from the '50s (Dion, Ricky Nelson, the Everly Brothers) mingled with the latest crop of pre-packaged Bobbys and Jimmys, while everyone waited for the real thing to come along.

HI FIDELITY — CP 444

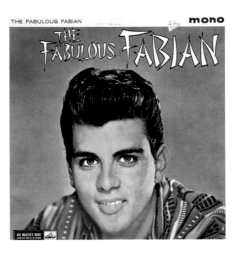

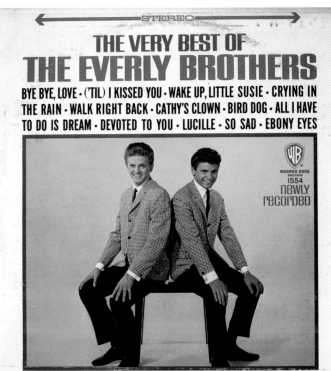

This 1968 vintage Gibson Everly
Brothers model is autographed
by Phil and Don.

EKS-74010 (stereo)

The Folkniks

The most baffling of the early '60s manias remains the folk or hootenanny craze. Concurrent with the Twist and right before surf music, everybody went wild for folk music. Well, some people called it folk music.

Popular groups like The Chad Mitchell Trio, Highwaymen and the Kingston Trio featured fresh-faced college boys in matching preppy ensembles, earnestly strumming white-bread renditions of "Good Night Irene." Things went from bad to worse when Mitch Miller and his "sing-along" gang got on the bandwagon.

Later, the Beatles-inspired British invasion introduced the cosmic hippie folk of Donovan and The Incredible String Band.

Remarkably, a few original talents emerged from the hootenanny hype. Bob Dylan, Fred Neil, Joan Baez and Eric Andersen made lasting contributions that were later integrated into the pop music mainstream via folk-rock.

In the late '80s, the Replacements paid homage, on the album *Hootenanny*, to the graphic style, if not the sound, of the original folkniks.

Eric Andersen 'bout changes & things

DESIGN: JULES HALFANT   PHOTO: JOEL BRODSKY

VANGUARD   RECORDINGS FOR THE CONNOISSEUR   VRS•9206

The Original

VOLUME 2

Hootenanny

America's Greatest Folksingers on One album with all the Excitement of a live Performance

GIBSON & CAMP Skillet Good and Greasy	THE LIMELITERS Lonesome Traveler	THEODORE BIKEL Poljushka
HOYT AXTON Downbound Train	JOSH WHITE Trouble	JUDY HENSKE Hooka Tooka	JUAN SERRANO Bulerias
DIAN & THE GREENBRIAR BOYS Sally Let Your Bangs Hang Down		CLARA WARD SINGERS I'm a Soldier	
ERIK DARLING Oh What A Beautiful City	YARBROUGH & CHILD Mary Had a Baby	THE TRAVELERS 3 Cotton Fields

The Replacements

Hootenanny

Lovelines	Treatment Bound	Buck Hill
Take Me Down to the Hospital	Run It	Mr. Whirly
Willpower	Color Me Impressed	You Lose
Within Your Reach	Hayday	Hootenanny

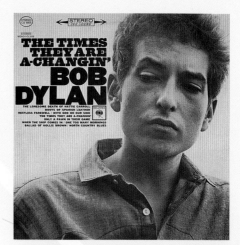

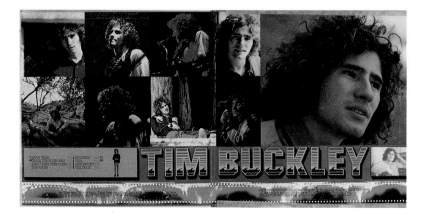

Shut Up and Act

In the '60s many singers attempted the transition from music to movies and TV, some with surprisingly strong results (Elvis, the Beatles, the Smothers Brothers and Bobby Darin come to mind).

Actors coveting music careers, however, are responsible for some of the most abysmal music of this or any decade. Wherever did record execs get the idea that because people enjoyed watching *Hogan's Heroes*, they would enjoy hearing them sing World War II songs?

At their best, these records achieve a weirdly amusing campiness that has endeared them to today's audiences through David Letterman's hilarious "Dave's Record Collection" segments.

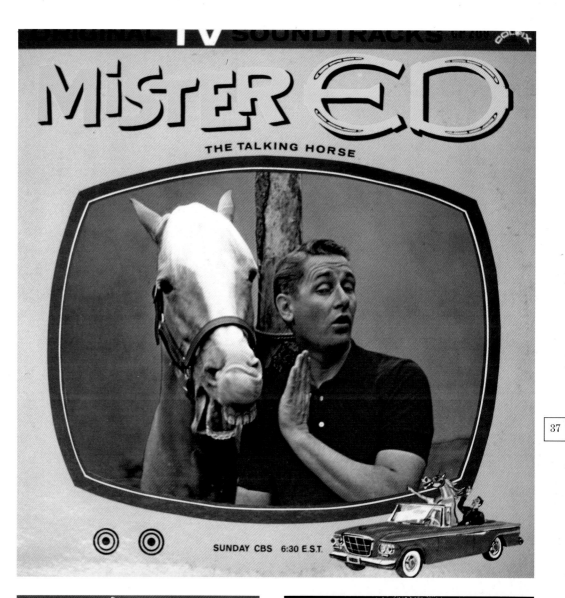

ORIGINAL TV SOUNDTRACKS

MISTER ED
THE TALKING HORSE

SUNDAY CBS 6:30 E.S.T.

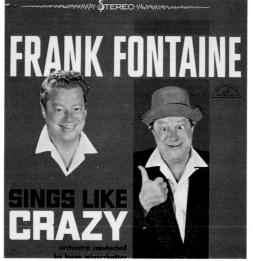

STEREO

FRANK FONTAINE

SINGS LIKE CRAZY

orchestra conducted by hugo winterhalter

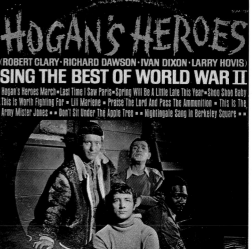

HOGAN'S HEROES
(ROBERT CLARY · RICHARD DAWSON · IVAN DIXON · LARRY HOVIS)
SING THE BEST OF WORLD WAR II
Hogan's Heroes March ▪ Last Time I Saw Paris ▪ Spring Will Be A Little Late This Year ▪ Shoo Shoo Baby ▪ This Is Worth Fighting For ▪ Lili Marlene ▪ Praise The Lord And Pass The Ammunition ▪ This Is The Army Mister Jones ▪ Don't Sit Under The Apple Tree ▪ ▪ Nightingale Sang In Berkeley Square ▪ ▪

LEONARD NIMOY THE WAY I FEEL

VINCENT EDWARDS Sings
STAR OF THE T V SHOW "BEN CASEY"

THE MAN FROM U.N.C.L.E. AND OTHER TV THEMES

RICHARD CHAMBERLAIN sings
(TV'S DR. KILDARE)

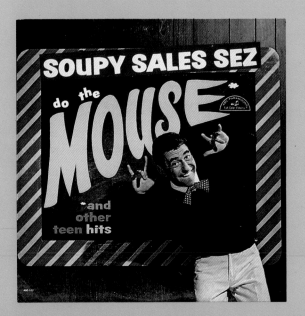

SOUPY SALES SEZ do the MOUSE and other teen hits

AL (HE'S THE KING) HIRT
THE HORN MEETS "THE HORNET"
GREEN HORNET THEME

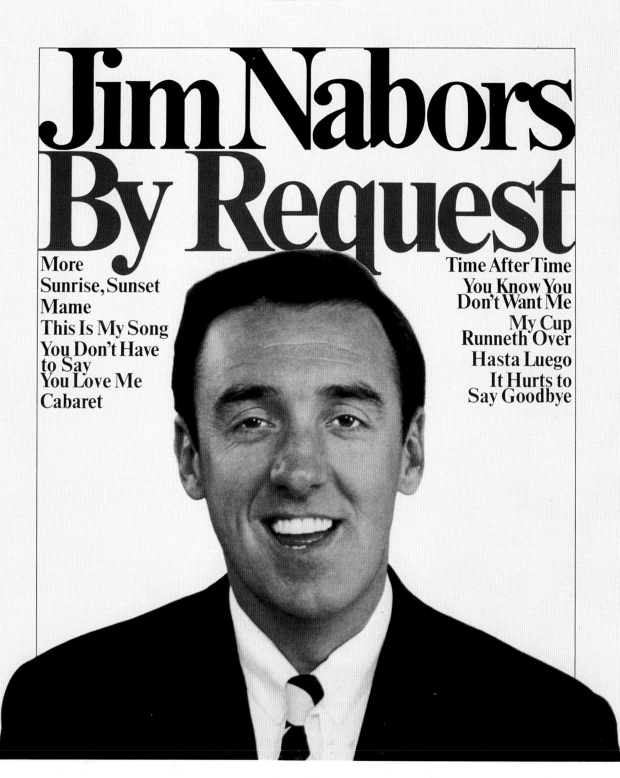

STEREO
360 SOUND

STEREO
CS 9465

CL 2665

COLUMBIA

Jim Nabors
By Request

More
Sunrise, Sunset
Mame
This Is My Song
You Don't Have
to Say
You Love Me
Cabaret

Time After Time
You Know You
Don't Want Me
My Cup
Runneth Over
Hasta Luego
It Hurts to
Say Goodbye

THE VENTURES
GREATEST HITS
VOLUME II

Sun, Fun, Cars and Guitars

Right after the Twist and just before the Beatles, America witnessed the surf and hot rod craze. What began as an innocent musical celebration of southern California's obsession with surfing and fast cars, soon grew into a national sensation.

Note the record by blues guitarist Freddy King on the next page. It is a prime example of how quick-buck operators deceptively packaged anything they could find as surf music. Instrumental rock, the guitar-dominated first cousin to surf music, represented by guitarists Dick Dale and Duane Eddy, drummer Sandy Nelson and groups like the Ventures and the Surfaris, was also extremely popular at the time.

While the rest of the surf groups are all but forgotten, Brian Wilson's music with the Beach Boys remains transcendent to this day.

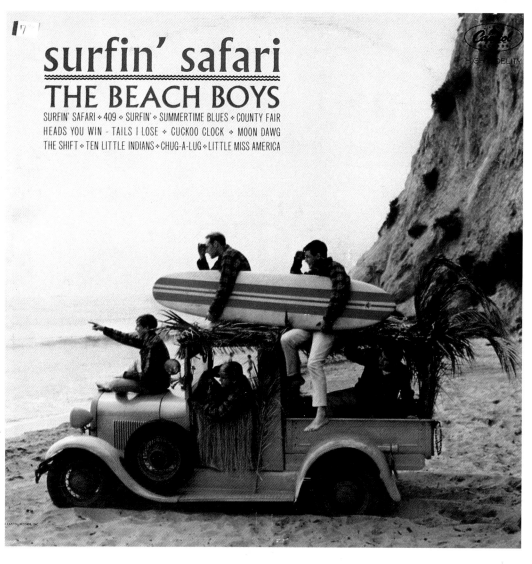

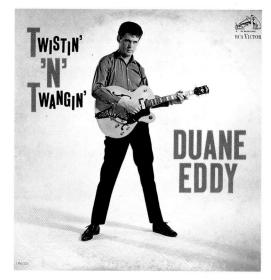

JAN & DEAN
surf city
And Other Swingin' Cities
DETROIT CITY   SOUL CITY
LIBERTY

I Left My Heart In
SAN FRANCISCO
SURF CITY
HONOLULU LULU
SOUL CITY   DETROIT CITY   MANHATTAN
PHILADELPHIA, PA.
You Came A Long Way From
ST. LOUIS   MEMPHIS
KANSAS CITY
Way Down Yonder In
NEW ORLEANS
TALLAHASSEE
LASSIE

LRP-3314

THE SURFARIS
THE ORIGINAL HIT VERSIONS!
Dot RECORDS
ULTRA HIGH-FIDELITY
WIPE OUT
AND
SURFER JOE
AND OTHER POPULAR SELECTIONS BY OTHER INSTRUMENTAL GROUPS

DLP 3535

freddy king
KING
856
Goes SURFIN'

THE HITS

Hide Away...The Stumble...San-Ho-Zay...Swooshy...Butterscotch...Side Tracked
Sen-Sa-Shun...Wash Out...In The Open...Heads Up...Just Pickin'...Out Front.

VIVID SOUND

5
6-8551
STEREO

soul surfin'
KAI WINDING
FEATURING KENNY BURRELL
HERO • SURF BIRD • TUBE WAIL • HEARSE RIDE • MORE (theme from Mondo Cane) • SPINNER
PIPELINE • COMIN' HOME BABY • GRAVY WALTZ • SUKIYAKA • SOUL SURFIN' • CHINA NIGHTS

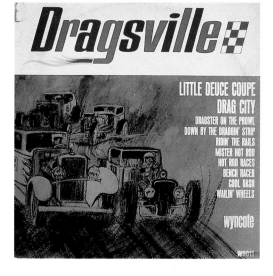

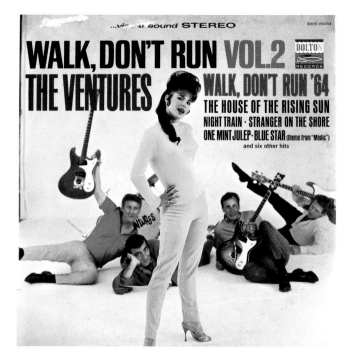

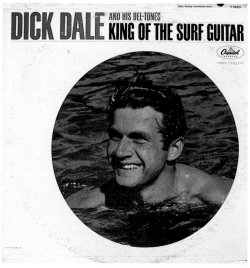

Surf music stars relied on guitars like this 1967 Mosrite Ventures model to achieve that legendary twangy sound.

HIGH FIDELITY
Demonstration
RECORD

Mercury
RECORDS
PJC-1

Music to live by

to fit your every mood, popular, jazz and classical,
through the magic of Mercury Living Presence Sound.

SUGGESTED RETAIL
$1.29
TAX INCLUDED

POPULAR

"NIGHT CAP"
RALPH MARTERIE
MG 20128 "Salute To The Aragon"

"NIGHTINGALE"
DICK CONTINO
MG 20141 "Something For The Girls"

"MY GAL SAL"
DAVID CARROLL
MG 20121 "Waltzes With David Carroll"

JAZZ

"ALL OF ME"
DINAH WASHINGTON (MG 36065)

"SEE MINOR"
JIMMY CLEVELAND (MG 36066)

"BOULEVARD OF BROKEN DREAMS"
TERRY GIBBS (MG 36064)

CLASSICAL EXCERPTS

CAPRICCIO ITALIEN (MG 50054)

TABUH-TABUHAN (MG 50103)

SCHUMAN SYMPHONY #2 (MG 50102)

BARTOK SECOND SUITE (MG 50098)

CHADWICK SYMPHONIC SKETCHES (MG 50104)

U. S. FIELD ARTILLERY MARCH (MG 50105)

Mom and Dad's Record Collection

If rock 'n' roll was for kids, what constituted "adult" music in the '60s? A quick flip through Mom and Dad's albums may shed some light.

Okay, so there's the occasional Broadway score or Christmas collection, but generally the evidence indicates that being a "sophisticated" adult in the '60s was all about enjoying sex, booze and cigarettes. Album jackets invoking fantasies of pagan sex in exotic locales are particularly abundant. Alcohol and nicotine being the World War II generation's drugs of choice, it's not much of a reach to the "sex, drugs and rock 'n' roll" of their children.

Featured here is the single most commonly occurring record in the known universe, Herb Alpert's *Whipped Cream and Other Delights*. This may not be the best selling record of all time, but it is most certainly the best selling record nobody wants. I once encountered 40 copies at a single charity thrift store. With its playful sexuality and thinly-veiled misogyny it's a classic '60s "Mom and Dad" design. The Pat Cooper and Soul Asylum records are just two of many spoofs done on the *Whipped Cream* theme.

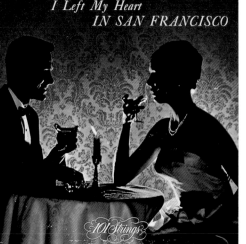

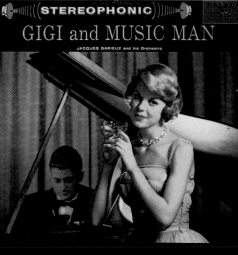

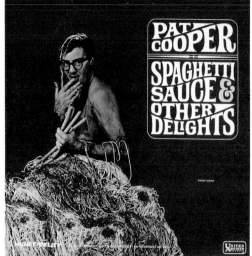

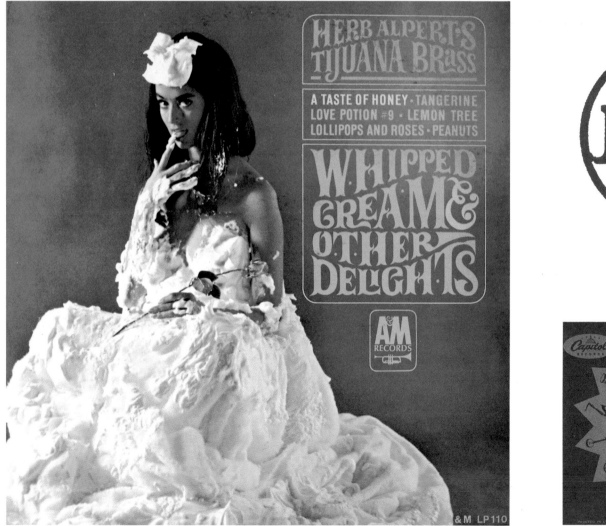

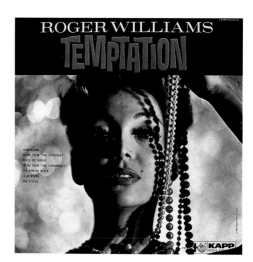

THE BEATLES' STORY

A NARRATIVE AND MUSICAL BIOGRAPHY OF BEATLEMANIA ON 2 LONG-PLAY RECORDS

includes
SELECTIONS FROM THEIR HIT RECORDS
INTERVIEWS WITH THE BEATLES AND THEIR FANS
MANY NEW PHOTOS
THEIR WHOLE STORY ON RECORD . . . FROM BEGINNING TO FABULOUS FAME!

Capitol
RECORDS

STEREO

Beatlemania

The biggest musical sensation of the '60s, The Beatles surprised everyone, including themselves, with the depth and breadth of their popularity. Obviously, the time was right, the talent was there and the rest is history.

At the height of Beatlemania all manner of Beatle paraphernalia was marketed. Fan mags, bubble gum cards, dashboard ornaments, lunch boxes, Beatle boots and even Beatle wigs were snatched up by eager fans of the Fab Four.

A few of the more notable collectibles featured here include the notorious *Yesterday And Today* "butcher" cover that owes its scarcity to a factory recall, and the legendary John and Yoko *Two Virgins* LP that featured a full-frontal nude portrait of the couple.

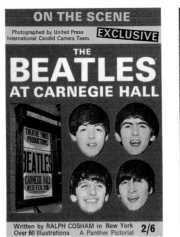

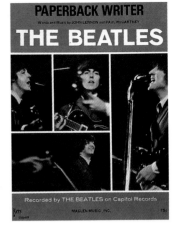

When fans tuned in the Ed Sullivan Show to catch The Beatles' first American TV appearance they saw George Harrison playing a Gretsch Country Gentleman guitar. The model pictured was featured in the 1962 Gretsch guitar catalog.

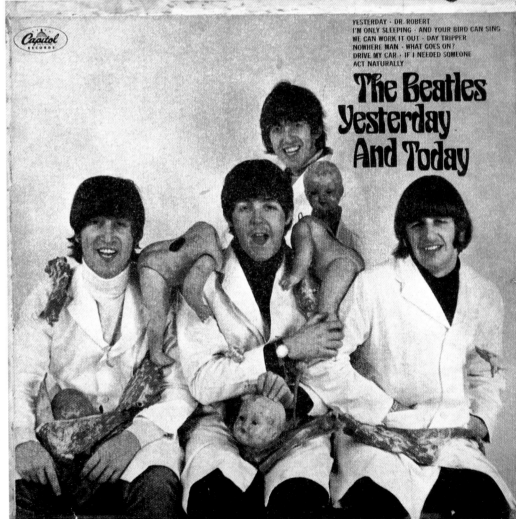

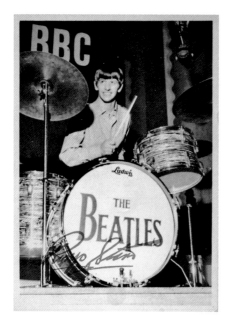

BEATLES

WHOLE TRUE STORY

16 SCOOP!

7 GIGANTIC COLOR PIN-UPS

100 HOT NEVER-BEFORE-SEEN PIX

WHERE THEY'LL STAY IN THE U.S. ● TOUR & TICKET INFO ● HOW YOU CAN MEET THEM!

39A *Beatles Diary*

Dear Diary,
Just before we appeared on the Ed Sullivan TV Show we received a telegram from Elvis Presley. This gave us a big lift, for we've all been fans of Elvis. Elvis wished us luck on our TV appearance and expressed the hope that the American public was as nice to us as the Britons have been to him. It was so thoughtful of him.

George

©T.C.G.   PRINTED IN U.S.A.

Wonderwall Music By George Harrison   Apple Records

This distinctive violin-shaped Hofner bass guitar (pictured is a model 500/1 from 1963) will forever be associated with Paul McCartney.

Selections by the Beatles plus original film music.

"When two great Saints meet it is a humbling experience. The long battles to prove he was a Saint."--Paul McCartney

Unfinished Music No. 1. Two Virgins. Yoko Ono/John Lennon.

Apple Records ● in association with Tetragrammaton Records. ⓟ T-5001 May 1968. Made in Merrie England.

This rare 1959 Rickenbacker model 315 is nearly identical to John Lennon's first electric guitar.

MONO

LL 3509

The Rolling Stones

Although they were destined for greater popularity and influence in the '70s, The Rolling Stones also made major contributions to the '60s, especially as a dirtier, scarier alternative to the cute and cuddly Beatles. Early on, they carved out a niche as the band your parents loved to hate. The Stones wrapped their albums in dark, brooding portraits and began perfecting a live show fraught with menace and bisexual allure.

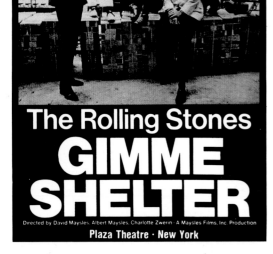

The British Invasion

The Beatles' American success opened the floodgates for British pop groups. Most were packaged as fun-loving mods in trendy matching suits. A visible minority took their cue from The Rolling Stones, appearing sullen and pouty, dressed in scruffy clothing. In the giddiness of the mid '60s it was impossible to predict which groups would make lasting contributions to rock 'n' roll.

Chuck Berry: St. Louis to Liverpool demonstrates that even influential American artists were not above jumping on the Merseybeat bandwagon. Your average '60s teen was blissfully unaware that it was Chuck Berry who had inspired the Beatles, and not the other way around.

CH 9186

CHUCK BERRY

LITTLE MARIE
YOU NEVER CAN TELL
NO PARTICULAR PLACE TO GO
GO, BOBBY SOXER
OUR LITTLE RENDEZ-VOUS
MERRY CHRISTMAS BABY
PROMISED LAND
THINGS I USED TO DO
LIVERPOOL DRIVE
NIGHT BEAT
YOU TWO
BRENDA LEE

ST. LOUIS TO LIVERPOOL

CHESS

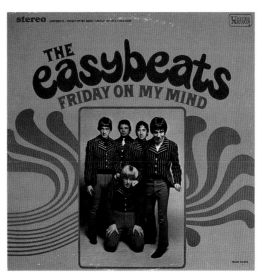

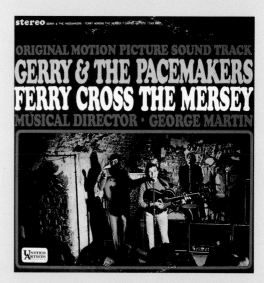

The Groupquake

The American response to the British invasion was not to fight them, but to join them. Angry suburban white kids emulating their favorite English groups spawned the first wave of garage rock. The earliest of these bands affected the mod look. Some, like Texas roots-rockers the Sir Douglas Quintet, went so far as to pass themselves off as Englishmen. Later on, the Anglophile groups were on the wane, eclipsed by a wave of home-grown psychedelia.

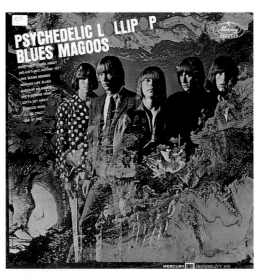

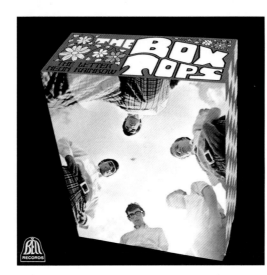

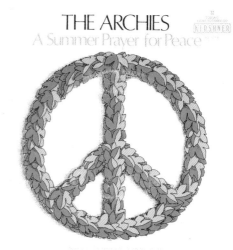

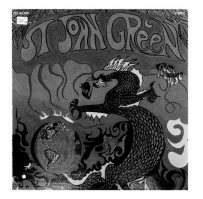

ELECTRIC BLUES —
CHICAGO STYLE

1. SNOOKY PRYOR Judgement Day
   (J. Pryor) Conrad Pub. Co. BMI 2:44
2. BILLY BOY ARNOLD You Got Me Wrong
   (J. Cryor) Tollie Music BMI 2:40
3. EDDIE TAYLOR Looking For Trouble
   (L. Harper) Conrad Pub. Co. BMI 2:26
4. BILLY BOY ARNOLD My Heart Is Crying
   (W. Arnold) Conrad Pub. Co. BMI 2:35
5. FLOYD JONES Any Old Lonesome Day
   (F. Jones) Conrad Pub. Co. BMI 2:58

SIDE 2   BDS 7511B

6. BILLY BOY ARNOLD Prisoner's Plea
   (W. Arnold) Conrad Pub. Co. BMI 2:57

BUDDAH RECORDS

SOPWITH CAMEL

P-8060

San Francisco

Local heroes Grateful Dead and Jefferson Airplane ushered in the psychedelic era around 1965, focusing international attention upon their Haight-Ashbury neighborhood.

The San Francisco scene was ultimately about much more than just alternative music. At its core was a new, experimental hippie society with its own politics, values and eclectic visual style.

Handbills and posters promoting acid-rock concerts at the Fillmore and the Avalon Ballroom helped to introduce this trippy new style of art and design. These colorful, densely-detailed and (to the uninitiated) nearly illegible posters established a visual vocabulary for the times.

Practitioners of these bold new graphics became cult artists in their own right, sharing fame if not fortune with the musicians they helped to promote.

Record packagers soon adopted the style, exposing important San Francisco artists Rick Griffin, Stanley Mouse, Victor Moscoso and Wes Wilson internationally. A curious blend of art nouveau, psychedilia, underground comix, Victorian typography and surfer mysticism, the San Francisco style was like nothing seen

before or since. No other music-related design approach has become so unequivocally associated with a specific musical genre.

All the examples featured here are originals from the '60s, excepting the *More American Graffiti* and *Nuggets* albums, both masterful examples of the San Francisco style's ability to evoke the psychedelic era.

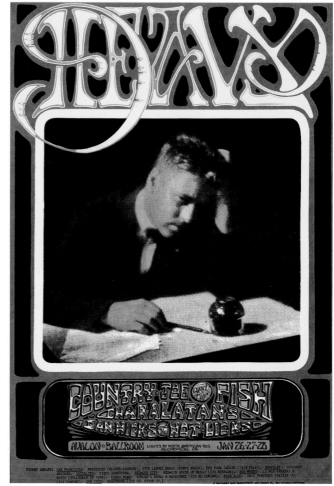

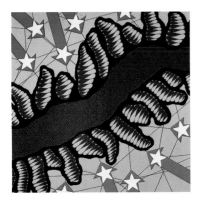

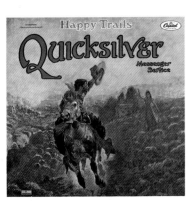

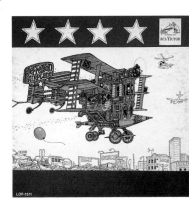

70

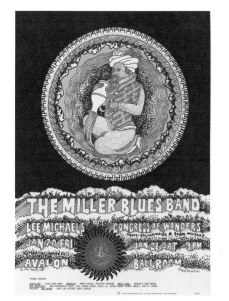

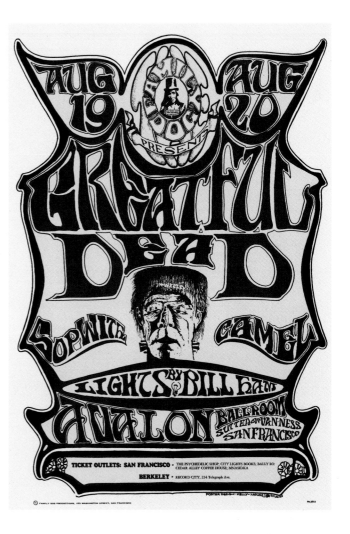

72

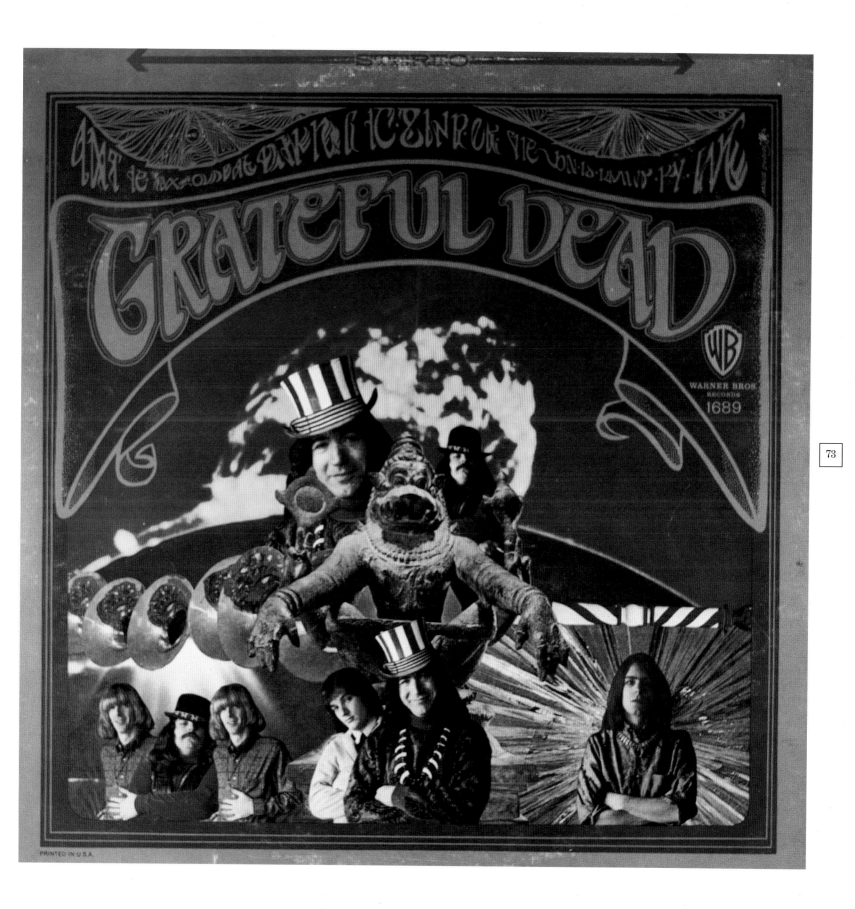

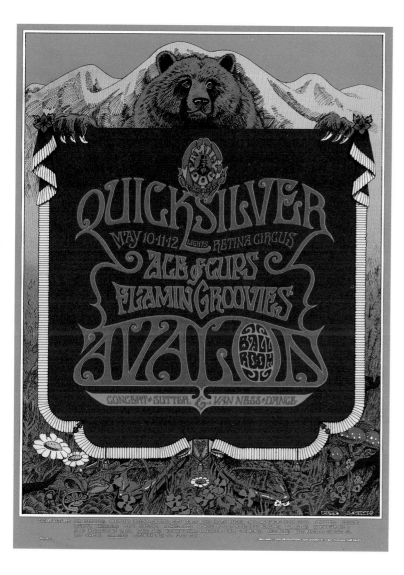

Perfectly Frank

Nothing was sacred to Frank Zappa, founder and resident genius of the Mothers of Invention. Suburbia, hippies, the establishment, groupies and even the Beatles were all fit subjects for Zappa's peculiar brand of satire.

Not afraid to bite the hand that feeds, Zappa singled out the music industry for particularly scathing criticism, eventually establishing his own record label, and signing an eccentric stable of artists. Iconoclastic graphics from Neon Park and Cal Schenkel perfectly captured the Zappa attitude, bringing a neo-dadaist ambiance to the packaging. These '60s Zappa records are highly collectible, owing no small part of their appeal to innovative graphic design.

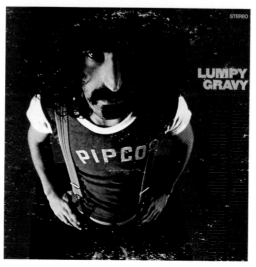

Something Fishy

What do Bob Dylan, the Beatles, Jimi Hendrix and Captain Beefheart have in common? They all appeared in "fish-eye" photos on their '60s album covers.

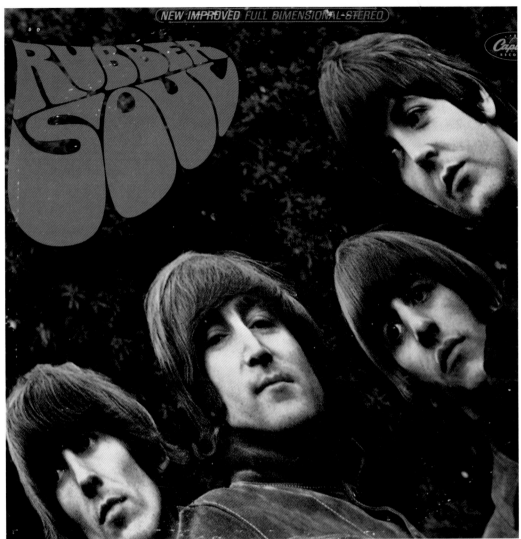

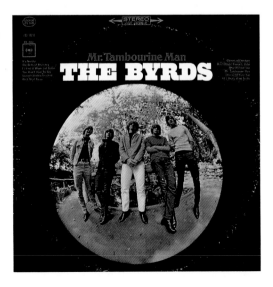

Modern Jazz

"Jazz design," typified by Reid Miles' modernist photographic covers for Blue Note, was solidly established at the start of the '60s, and variations on that style persisted through mid-decade. Abstract expressionism, considered too far out in the '50s, was now acceptable, and found its way onto many early '60s jazz sleeves.

Although 1962's Bossa Nova craze gave the music a brief commercial boost, the audience for jazz was a devoted but comparatively tiny one. It wasn't until the first rumblings of jazz-rock fusion at the decade's end that the music would find a wider audience. The *Gary Burton Quartet in Concert* cover is typical of the psychedelic designs used to package late '60s fusion records for jazz's newly-expanded constituency.

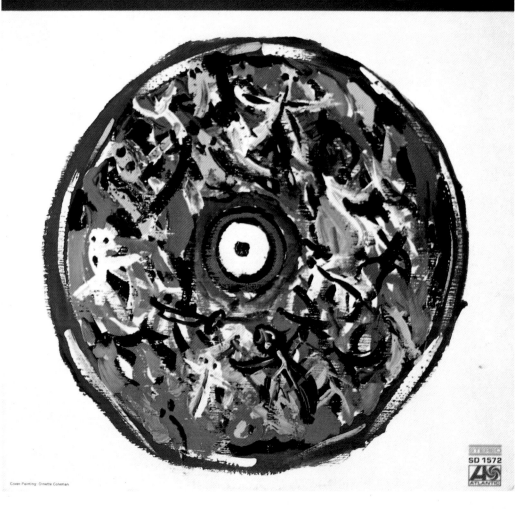

Ornette Coleman / The Art of The Improvisers

Cover Painting: Ornette Coleman

STEREO
SD 1572
ATLANTIC

HIGH FIDELITY
Discuba
LPD 557
ALTA FIDELIDAD

Ja-Ja-Pachá

Orquesta Aragón

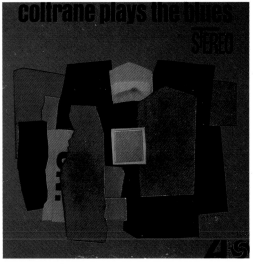

coltrane plays the blues

STEREO

SD 1419

coltrane's sound

TIME CHANGES
THE DAVE BRUBECK QUARTET

herbie
mann at the
village
gate
STEREO

PRESTIGE

Components
Bobby
Hutcherson

FREDDIE HUBBARD/JAMES SPAULDING/HERBIE HANCOCK/RON CARTER/JOE CHAMBERS

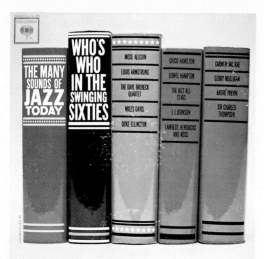

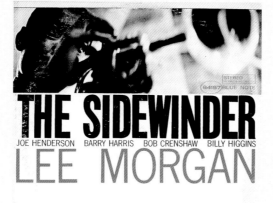

THE SIDEWINDER
JOE HENDERSON   BARRY HARRIS   BOB CRENSHAW   BILLY HIGGINS
LEE MORGAN

CANNONBALL & COLTRANE

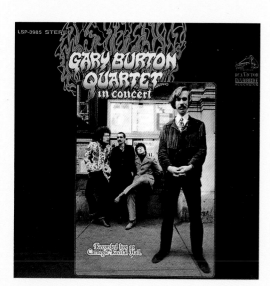

GARY BURTON QUARTET in concert

Recorded live at Carnegie Recital Hall.

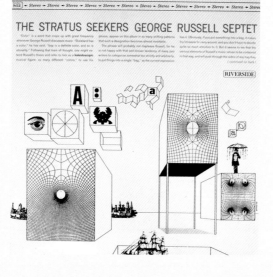

THE STRATUS SEEKERS GEORGE RUSSELL SEPTET

RIVERSIDE

PHILIPS

This Gibson model L5CES from 1961 is the type that Wes Montgomery used to forge his signature sound.

Cecil Taylor

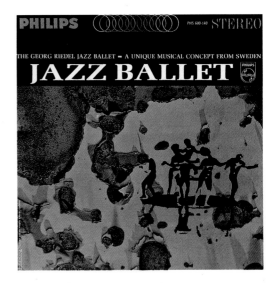

Blues and Rhythm

When packaging blues for the black audience, most labels opted for the low-budget generic graphics of *Freddy King Sings*. Circa 1960 the recording industry found that blues could be marketed, with appropriate graphics, to the Ivy League as a part of the folk and hootenanny craze. By the decade's end marketers had to update their approach, dressing the blues in psychedelic garb to lure the college crowd.

HIGH FIDELITY
KING
762

FREDDY KING SINGS

LONESOME WHISTLE BLUES
YOU'VE GOT TO LOVE HER WITH A FEELING
HAVE YOU EVER LOVED A WOMAN
YOU KNOW THAT YOU LOVE ME (But You Never Tell Me So)
YOU MEAN, MEAN WOMAN (How Can Your Love Be True)
IT'S TOO BAD THINGS ARE GOING SO TOUGH
IF YOU BELIEVE (In What You Do)
LET ME BE (Stay Away From Me)
TAKIN' CARE OF BUSINESS
I LOVE THE WOMAN
I'M TORE DOWN
SEE SEE BABY

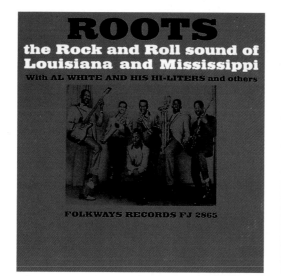

ROOTS
the Rock and Roll sound of
Louisiana and Mississippi
With AL WHITE AND HIS HI-LITERS and others

FOLKWAYS RECORDS FJ 2865

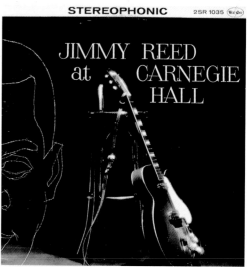

STEREOPHONIC   2SR 1035

JIMMY REED at CARNEGIE HALL

Jewel...... RECORDS

IMPERIAL

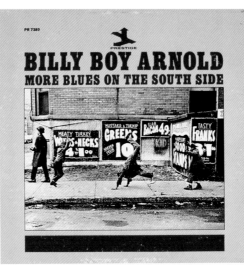

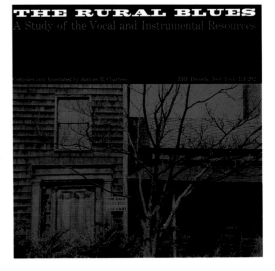

90

MUDDY WATERS
Down on Stovall's Plantation
His First Recordings—The Historic
1941-42 Library of Congress Recordings

Specialty

SP-586-45

Pub: Venice-BMI
Time: 2:20

STEPPIN' HIGH
(Allen-Tyler)

EDGAR BLANCHARD
And His Band

STAX S 723   STEREO

FRIDAY
13

ALBERT
KING
BORN
UNDER A
BAD SIGN

A
A

Stax

SLIM HARPO
RAININ'
IN MY
HEART

COMPATIBLE STEREO

EXCELLO

ARHOOLIE

ACE RECORDS

The nickel-plated National steel guitars used in the '60s by blues men Son House and Johnny Winter were actually manufactured in the '20s and '30s. Shown is an exquisite National style 4 from 1929, miraculously preserved in mint condition.

REGULAR
CL 1464

COLUMBIA
GUARANTEED HIGH FIDELITY

JOHNNY CASH
RIDE
THIS
TRAIN

FEATURING
THE SMASH HIT
"GOING TO
MEMPHIS"

A Stirring Travelogue
of America
in Song and Story

LOADING COAL
SLOW RIDER
LUMBERJACK
DORRAINE OF PONCHARTRAIN
GOING TO MEMPHIS
WHEN PAPA PLAYED THE DOBRO
BOSS JACK
OLD DOC BROWN

Country Western

Regrettably, the major labels didn't put much time or design effort into their '60s country record sleeves. Most were given a kind of B-movie packaging, relying heavily on the obvious clichés like trucks, trains and cowboys. The resulting covers were virtually interchangeable, even for important artists like Johnny Cash and Merle Haggard, who certainly deserved better. *Sweetheart of the Rodeo* by the Byrds showcased the visionary country rock of Gram Parsons and gave the world a glimpse of things to come in the '70s.

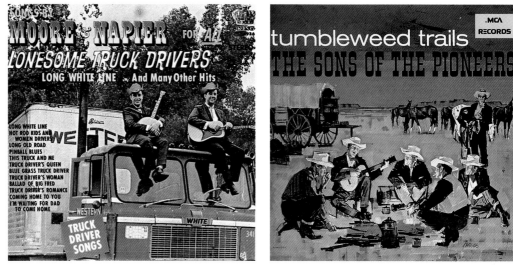

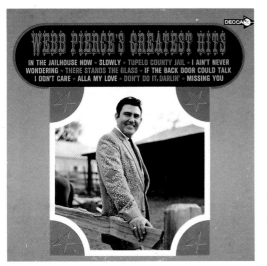

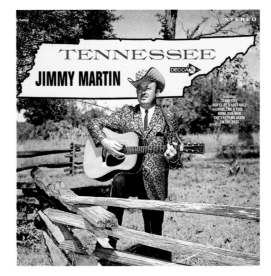

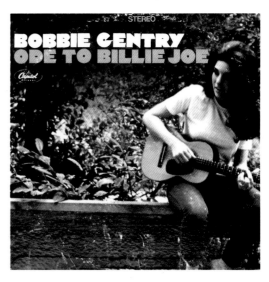

The Fender Telecaster Custom, like the 1961 model pictured here, was popular with '60s country pickers.

This 1961 Gretsch White Falcon, with its gold-plated Cadillac tailpiece, typifies the flashy guitars preferred by country stars in the '60s.

Sweet Soul Music

At the start of the '60s Black music was known as rhythm and blues, but after assimilating the powerful influence of gospel music it was born again and rechristened soul music. Several regional styles emerged simultaneously: the uptown soul of New York, Detroit's pop-gospel Motown sound, and the red clay soul of Memphis and Muscle Shoals.

The typical '60s soul record jacket design was pure hard sell. More than any other '60s music, these LPs seem to have a strong kinship with grocery store packages. Soul designers used the same bold graphics and attention-getting devices more commonly seen on boxes of Post Toasties and Tide. It wasn't until the dawn of the '70s that the self-consciously arty influence of the psychedelic style found its way onto the covers of soul records.

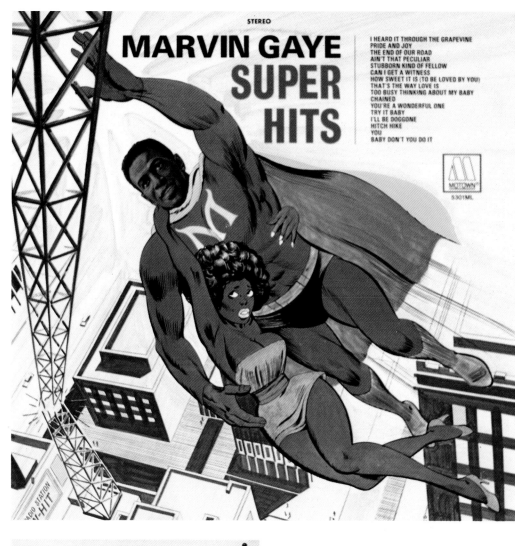

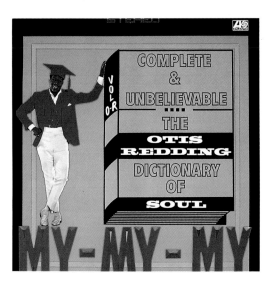

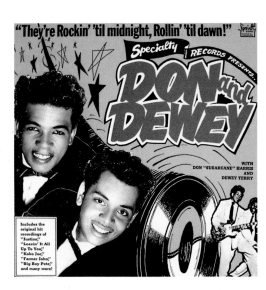

THE FAMOUS ISLEY BROTHERS *Twisting and Shouting*

SE-4332 STEREO

The Royalettes
It's Gonna Take A Miracle
Arranged and produced by TEDDY RANDAZZO

DON'T THROW YOUR LOVE AWAY
the Orlons
CAMEO
C-287

R I C

STAX

103

ARTHUR CONLEY
MORE SWEET SOUL

ATLANTIC
45 R.P.M.
45-2221
VOCAL
Pub. Picturetone
Mellin, BMI
Time: 2:53
A-7527
Directed By BERT BERNS
MY GIRL SLOOPY
(Berns - Farrell)
THE VIBRATIONS
Arr. & Cond. by Teacho Wilshire
An Award Music Production

ZIP-A-DEE DOO DAH
BOB-B-SOXX AND THE BLUE JEANS

SOUL SISTER, BROWN SUGAR
COME ON IN

Congratulations from
Stax/Volt, SOULSVILLE, U.S.A.
the BIG sound of '67

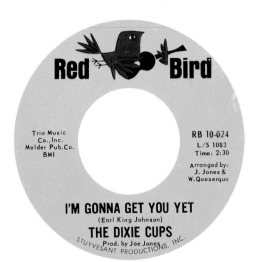

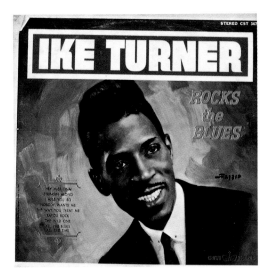

PRISONER OF LOVE

JAMES BROWN

KING
851

NIXON'S THE ONE

NIXON THE ONE

NIXON'S THE ONE

EXCERPTS FROM
RICHARD M. NIXON'S
NOMINATION ACCEPTANCE SPEECH
AUGUST 8, 1968

Play manually at 33⅓
Keep record as flat as poss

auravision ©
AN ACTIVITY OF COLUMBIA SPECIAL PRODUCTS
A PRODUCT OF CBS RECORDS

Where the Reaction Is

The '60s conservative backlash proves that for every action there is a reaction. While most music-biz insiders were associated with anti-establishment and anti-Vietnam sentiments, the industry's right wing retaliated with Sergeant Barry Sadler, Anita Bryant and the candy-coated pieties of Up With People. In hindsight, it all seems rather laughable. I mean, the Grateful Dead vs. Up With People? No contest.

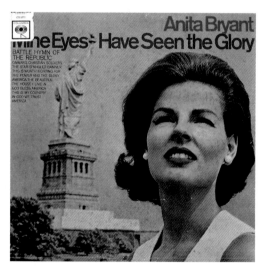

All The News That Fits

Pop music's influence was pervasive in '60s culture, extending to movies, TV and especially the print media. The era's underground newspapers and comix featured the same visual artists (R. Crumb, Rick Griffin, Victor Moscoso) that contributed posters and record sleeve designs to the music scene, as well as continuing journalistic coverage of alternative music and its purveyors.

On November 9, 1967 *Rolling Stone* debuted in San Francisco. It may not have been the first, but it is certainly the most influential and longest-running of the new rock journals launched in the '60s. Now based in New York City, *Rolling Stone* thrives today, its format having evolved to encompass pop culture, politics, movies and TV, as well as music.

Recognize Private Gripeweed? He's actually John Lennon in Richard Lester's new film, How I Won the War. An illustrated special preview of the movie begins on page 16.

THE HIGH COST OF MUSIC AND LOVE: WHERE'S THE MONEY FROM MONTEREY?

BY MICHAEL LYDON

A weekend of "music, love, and flowers" can be done for a song (plus cost) or can be done at a cost (plus songs). The Monterey International Pop Festival, a non-profit, charity event, was, despite its own protestations, of the second sort: a damn extravagant three days.

The Festival's net profit at the end of August, the last date of accounting, was $211,451. The costs of the weekend were $290,233. Had it not been for the profit from the sale of television rights to ABC/TV of $288,843, the whole operation would have ended up a neat $77,392 in the red.

The Festival planned to have all the artists, while in Monterey, submit ideas for use of the proceeds.

In the confusion the plan miscarried and the decision on where the profits should go has still not been finally made.

So far only $50,000 has definitely been been allocated to anyone: to a unit of the New York City Youth Board which will set up classes for many ghetto children to learn music on guitars donated by Fender. Paul Simon, a Festival governor, will personally over-see the program.

Plans to give more money to the Negro College Fund for college scholarships is now being discussed, another idea is a sum between ten and twenty thousand for the Monterey Symphony.

However worthy these plans, they are considerably less daring and innovative than the projects mentioned in the spring: the Diggers, pop conferences, and any project which would "tend to further national interest in and knowledge and enjoyment of popular music." The present plans suggest that the Board of Governors, unable or unwilling to make their grandiose schemes reality, fell back on traditional charity.

The Board of Governors did decide that the money would be given out in a small number of large sums. This has meant, for instance, that the John Edwards Memorial Foundation, a folk music archive at the University of California at Los Angeles, got its small request overlooked.

In ironic fact, what happened at the Festival and its financial affairs looks in many ways like the traditional Charity Ball in hippie drag.

The overhead was high and the net was low. "For every dollar spent, there was a reason," says Derek Taylor, the Festival's PR man and one of its original officers.

Yet many of the Festival's expenses, however reasonable to Taylor, seem out of keeping with its announced spirit. The Festival management, with amateurish good will, lavished generosity on their friends.

• Producer Lou Adler was able to find a spot in the show for his own property, Johnny Rivers; Paul Simon for his friend, English folk singer Beverly; Ann Phillips for the Group Without A Name and Scott MacKenzie. None of them had the musical

Tom Rounds Quits KFRC

Tom Rounds, KFRC Program Director, has resigned. No immediate date has been set for his departure from the station. Rounds quit to assume the direction of Charlatan Productions, an L.A. based film company experimenting in the contemporary pop film.

Rounds spent seven years as Program Director of KPOI in Hawaii before coming to San Francisco in 1966. He successfully effected the tight format which made KFRC the number one station in San Francisco.

Les Turpin, former program director of KGB in San Diego will replace Tom Rounds at KFRC. Turpin has spent the last year as a consultant in the Drake-Chenault programming service.

The new appointment could mean a tightening up of programming policies. Rounds liberalization of KFRC's play-list may well become more restricted.

Airplane high, but no new LP release

Jefferson Airplane has been taking more than a month to record their new album for RCA Victor. In a recording period of five weeks only five sides have been completed. No definite release date has been set.

Its usual recording schedule begins at 11:00 p.m. in the evening and extends through six or seven in the morning. When they're not in the studios, they stay at a fabulous mansion which rents for $5,000 a month. The Beatles stayed at the house on their last American tour.

The house has two swimming pools and a variety of recreational facilities. It's a small little paradise in the hills above Hollywood. Maybe suntans and guitars don't make it together.

status for an international pop music festival.

It is ironic that the Rivers and the rest appeared "free," but the money it cost the Festival to get them to Monterey and back, feed them, put them up (Beverly
—Continued on Page 7

—Continued on Page 7

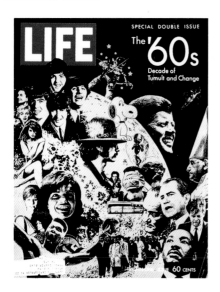

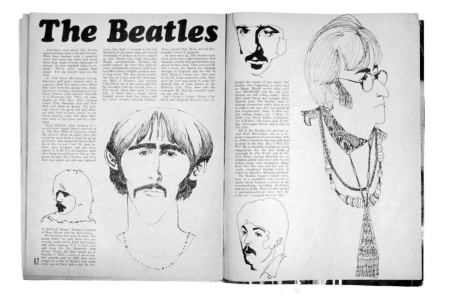

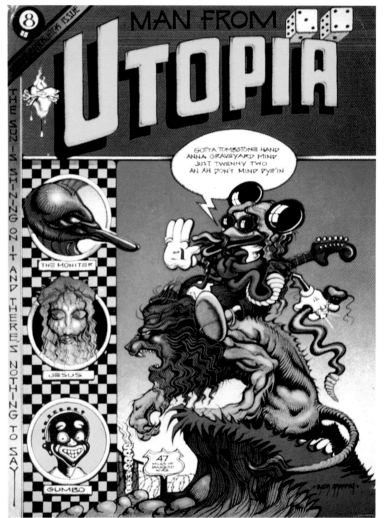

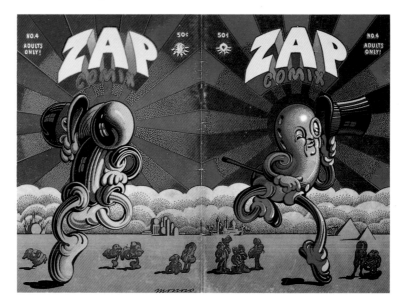

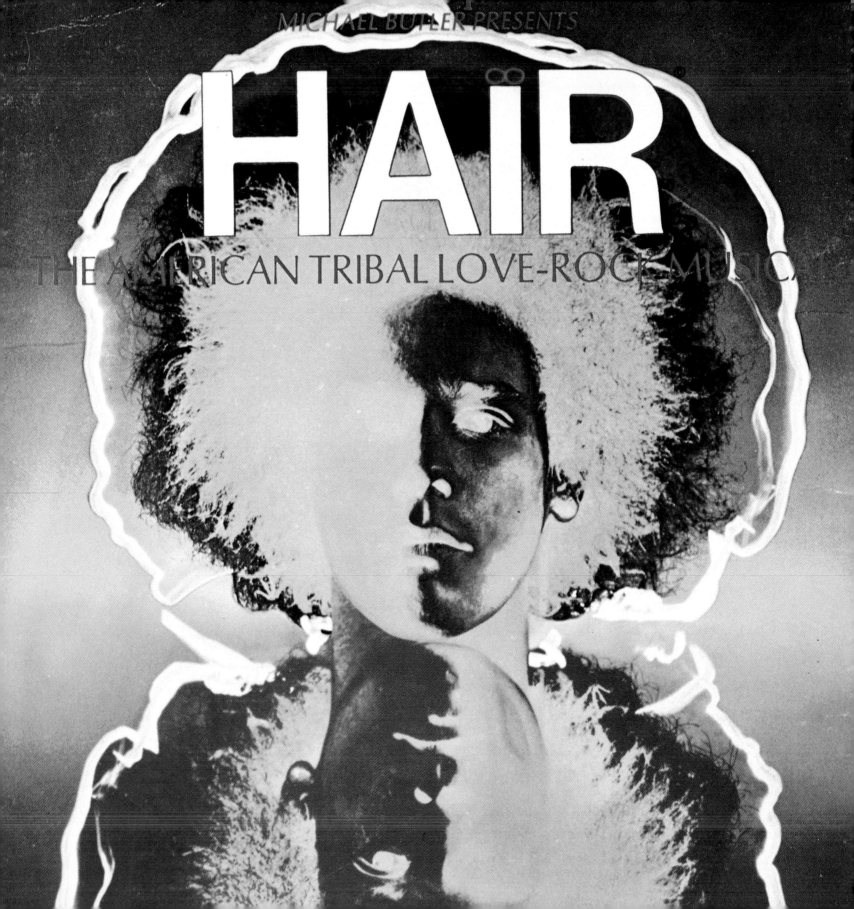

Live and On Stage

Shows, concerts and festivals provided gathering places for '60s music fans to see and hear music previously experienced only through radio and records. The immensely popular 1969 Woodstock Music and Art Fair took everyone by surprise, establishing once and for all that rock was here to stay.

Great Pretenders

Throughout the mid '60s, deceptively packaged "greatest hits" knock-offs were everywhere. While there were many legitimate offerings containing authentic hit songs performed by the original artists (*Super Hits Vol. 3, 24 Dynamic Hits*), they were nearly indistinguishable amidst the deluge of cheesy knock-offs. Buyer beware: If you didn't take time to read the fine print you might mistakenly purchase *Hank Williams (sung by Jug Scott)* or the Guadalajara Brass when you really wanted the Tijuana Brass. Can you imagine today's CD buyers falling for *The Best of REM (sung by DUI)*? How could '60s consumers have been so gullible?

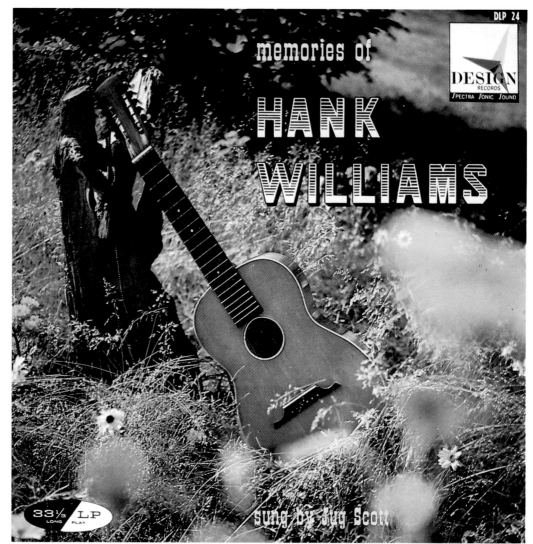

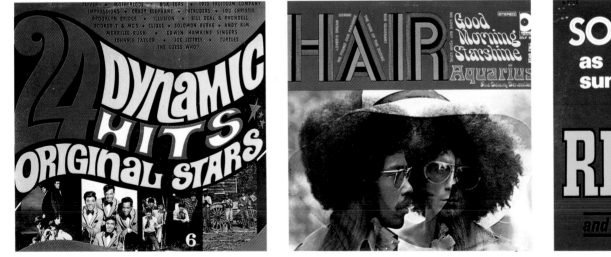

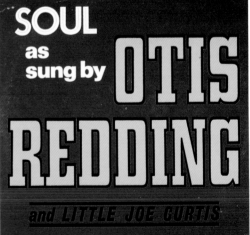

STEREO
SPC-

HEY JUDE
THOSE WERE THE DAYS
ABRAHAM, MARTIN & JOHN
STORMY
FOR ONCE IN MY LIFE
CHEWY, CHEWY
I LOVE HOW YOU LOVE ME
BOTH SIDES NOW
KENTUCKY WOMAN
TOO WEAK TO FIGHT
BONUS! ORIGINAL GOLDEN OLDIE
WILBERT HARRISON
KANSAS CITY

pickwick/33 RECORDS

A PRODUCT OF
PICKWICK
INTERNATIONAL,
INC.

Where the Wild Things Are

If this book has sparked your interest in collecting '60s music memorabilia, or maybe you're just interested in assessing the value of your dusty collection of '60s era LPs and 45s (don't get your hopes up, relatively few records have serious monetary value), we have compiled this listing of music collectibles resources.

Periodicals

Goldmine
(twice monthly)
700 E. State St.
Iola, WI 54990
715-445-2214

Discoveries
(monthly)
Jelly Roll Publications
Box 255
Port Townsend, WA 98368
206-385-1200

These two publications specialize in music memorabilia with an emphasis on records and compact discs. They are a treasure trove of mail auctions, pricing and swap meet dates and locations.

Price Guides

Collecting the Beatles
Barbara Fenick
Contemporary Books

Psychedelic Collectibles of the 1960s & 1970s
An Illustrated Price Guide
Susanne White
Wallace-Homestead Books

Rockin' Records Price Guide
Jerry P. Osborne
Jelly Roll Publications

Goldmine's Price Guide to Collectible Record Albums
Neal Umphred
Krause Publications

Bibliography

Rare Records Wax Trash & Vinyl Treasures
Tom Hibbert
Proteus Books

Research #14: Incredibly Strange Music, Vols. 1 & 2
Re/Search Publications

Journey to the Center of the Garage
A Guide to Obscure American Psychedelic Punk Bands of the Sixties
Beverly Paterson
Emerald Publications

Museums & Exhibits

The **Rock and Roll Hall of Fame** *is due to open in Cleveland, Ohio in 1995.*

The **Hard Rock Cafe**'s *extensive collection of pop music memorabilia is on public display in their numerous restaurants located in major cities worldwide.*

Retailers

Of records, books and other music collectibles:

Kelly's Klassics
Kelly Massing, *proprietor*
2184 Wilton Drive
Fort Lauderdale, FL 33305
305-568-2580

The Incredible Record & Book Store
Jonathan Lipsin, *proprietor*
778 Yonge Street
Toronto, Canada M4Y 2C1
416-924-8881

Classic Pre-owned Guitars

The Guitar Broker
Craig Brody, *proprietor*
2455 East Sunrise Blvd.
Fort Lauderdale, FL 33304
305-563-5507

'60s Music Posters

Postermat
Poster Art of the 60s
401 Columbus Avenue
San Francisco, CA 94133
415-421-5536

Psychedelic Solution Gallery
33 West Eighth Street, 2nd Floor
New York, NY 10011
212-529-2462

INDEX

Album Titles

Recording Artists

ACKNOWLEDGMENTS

Thanks to Phil Skinner of Pompano Beach, Florida, for the photos he took of Craig Brody's guitar collection and to Noah Otalvro of Vogue Photography in Miami, and Tom Simon of T. Simon Photography in Cuyahoga Falls, Ohio, for photographing all the other objects featured in this book.

Thank you to Andrew Bing, Kenny Winston, Judy Borich, Brian Lazar, Marilyn Esposito and Tom Simon for sharing their private collections.

Special thanks to Kelly Massing of Kelly's Klassics in Fort Lauderdale, Jonathan Lipsin of The Incredible Record & Book Store in Toronto, and Craig Brody of The Guitar Broker in Fort Lauderdale for their advice, patience, enthusiasm, and access to their stores.

Thank you to John Brady for his advice and patience during the preparation of this book and to Cheryl Frost for production assistance.

Special thanks to Peter Noone for his kind words in the Foreword.

For their support and encouragement I would like to thank the staff at PBC International: Publisher, Mark Serchuck; Managing Director, Penny Sibal; Technical Director, Richard Liu; Managing Editor, Susan Kapsis; and Assistant Editor, Francine Hornberger. Thanks to Garrett Schuh for his cover and interior page designs.

My boundless gratitude goes out to the often anonymous designers, photographers and illustrators whose vision we celebrate in this book, and the musicians who inspired them.